Published by
PAVIC Publications
Library & Learning Resources
Sheffield Hallam University

Design & Typesetting by
Graphics Unit
Library & Learning Resources
Sheffield Hallam University

Printed by
Print Unit
Sheffield Hallam University

PAVIC Publications
Library and Learning Resources

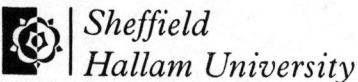

© 1994 ISBN 0 86339 4132

Politics in the 'Nineties

Series Editor; Duncan Watts, Editor of PARC
Titles in Series

About
POLITICS IN THE 'NINETIES

This series aims to cover a range of topics frequently discussed in the study of British Government and Politics. The booklets are intended to be comprehensive, stimulating and up-to-date.

They can be used for reference on particular aspects of the subject or to provide a sufficiently thorough review of the material as to enable an 'A' level candidate to find out most of what needs to be known. Deliberately, there is not a definite conclusion to be found at the end; rather, in the light of the selection of material presented, it is hoped that the reader will be able to formulate his/her own judgements.

It is hoped that others might find the information presented helpful to them. First year students in Higher Education may well be able to obtain the basis of their knowledge from these booklets. Teachers and lecturers, not only in the field of Government but also of General and Liberal Studies, may also find them a useful sourcebook.

It is up to the reader to extract what is wanted from the content, either a full review of the topic explored, or facts and figures needed in the pursuit of their enquiries. The format generally allows chapters to be read as part of the whole, or in isolation.

About the Author

Duncan Watts is the Editor of the Politics Association Resource Centre. He was an 'A' level teacher for many years in both a Grammar and a Comprehensive School. He now tutors part-time in Politics and in Modern History, and is also an examiner and writer. He has written a biography of Joseph Chamberlain and an analysis of Nineteenth Century Conservatism, and is currently compiling a history of the Liberal Party.

CONTENTS

List of Tables

Introduction

Tackling the subject of our basic rights inevitably involves problems of selection, definition and evaluation. In this booklet, there is no attempt to cover the world-wide problem of human rights and the all-too-frequent denial of them. Here, we are concerned with our liberties in Britain, and whether they need to be given more assured protection.

Britain was a signatory to the Universal Declaration of Human Rights, adopted by the United Nations General Assembly on December 10th 1948. This dealt with two types of rights, civil and political, and economic and social, and though the document has no legal status it stands as an ideal to which all members should aspire.

In 1953, there followed the Council of Europe's European Convention on Human Rights and this has provided many useful opportunities for maintaining freedom, especially the liberty of the individual and the rights of minorities. Its example has impressed many lawyers throughout the world, as was clear at New Delhi (1959) when the International Commission of Jurists urged all governments to draw inspiration from the European example.

This European Convention, and the machinery which enforces it, has nothing to do with the European Community. Thus the European Court at Strasbourg is not to be confused with the Court of Justice at Luxembourg which deals with EC law.

Similarly, to avoid confusion, the Bill of Rights discussed here is not connected with the one enacted in 1689. That legislation followed in the aftermath of the Glorious Revolution of the previous year, and was concerned with the relationship of Parliament and the Crown. The Bill referred to in this booklet is concerned with human rights, and the provision of a document comprehensively enumerating them as a basic part of our constitutional arrangements.

The relationship between the individual and the state is a complex one. The citizen expects to enjoy certain basic rights, including the freedom to do certain things and the freedom from having some things done to him or her. Both types of freedom are valuable, but such individual freedoms have to be balanced by an acknowledgement of the rights of the state to act on behalf of the entire community.

At present, the basis of our civil rights is in some ways precarious, in that we do not have a written constitution which codifies what those rights are. If we did have such a document, it would enshrine such elementary principles as freedom of assembly, freedom of speech, and the principle of innocence before the law until proven guilty. It is claimed by defenders of the present situation that our civil rights are already adequately defended in British law by our existing arrangements.

This claim has been much disputed in recent years, for many people believe that our rulers have been chipping away at our basic freedoms. In this discussion of our rights and recent threats to them, it is the present Government's policies which are often alluded to. This happens to be a Conservative administration but any government so long in office might show signs of riding roughshod over opposition. Such is the arrogance of power.

Chapter One

The Rights of the Citizen in Britain

It is often claimed that the individual citizen in Britain probably has more freedoms than in any other country. These have been an important part of our long tradition of stability and political liberty, yet these rights rest essentially on the age-old assumption by British courts that a person may do as he/she likes providing that this does not involve a breach of any particular law; in other words, we can do or say what we wish, provided it is not specifically forbidden.

Almost along among democratic countries, we do not have a written constitution; where these exist, they often provide for 'fundamental rights' of the individual. As our rights are not gathered together in such a document, our liberty rests on a different basis from elsewhere. We have enjoyed the rule of law for at least 300 years and our rights have been established not primarily by the proclamations of politicians, but by judicial decisions in which judges have interpreted the Common Law of the Land.

As our rights are not stated in laws directly proclaiming them, their extent can only be assessed by considering particular types of freedoms and the limitations which have developed over the years on the exercise of them.

Basic Freedoms

In any country calling itself democratic, certain fundamental freedoms are necessary and would, in principle, command ready agreement. When people also claim additional social rights, such as the right to work or the right to strike, then one enters the realms of controversy.

Despite such difficulties, we can proceed to examine the sort of protection the citizen may expect to enjoy.

1. THE RIGHT TO VOTE IN FREE ELECTIONS. Free elections may be regarded as a litmus test for democracy. The right of all qualified adults to vote is therefore a basic one; there is no test of fitness or literacy, no disqualification on grounds of race nor of religion. Providing that the person is a British citizen, 18 or older, resident in a constituency and not subject to a disability such as certified insanity, confinement in prison or membership of the House of Lords, then he/she may vote.

2. An obvious prerequisite for free elections is freedom of expression, THE RIGHT TO SPEAK AND WRITE FREELY. The limits placed upon what may be said and written are not

very stringent and do not forbid the expression of opinions critical of the Crown or of the government. Fascist, Communist or Anarchist speakers are all free to express their viewpoint subject only to not inciting people to acts of violence or to racial hatred.

As with other freedoms, we have no special protection to enable us to speak freely but there are no restrictions to interfere with our rights unless we fall foul of particular laws. The main constraints are:

a) The Law of Sedition. The definition of seditious libel was originally a far-reaching one but prosecutions in the C20 have been very rare for such offences, and juries are unwilling to convict for the expression of opinion on public affairs. The modern interpretation of sedition is narrow and it allows the most fundamental and hostile criticism of the organisation of society and the system of government. Mr. Justice Coleridge (the King V Aldred 1909) defined it as language calculated 'to incite others to public disorder, to wit, rebellions, insurrections, assassinations, outrages or any physical force or violence of any kind.'

b) The Law of Blasphemy is a further limitation and in bygone days any attack on Christianity was thought to be blasphemous: In the C20 it has been interpreted much more narrowly and is therefore an uncommon offence. It has, however, been invoked successfully in a prosecution against the then editor of Gay News, Derek Lemon. In 1977, he published a poem, 'The Love that Dares to Speak its Name' and an accompanying drawing, which were held 'to vilify Christ in His Life and His Crucifixion.'

c) The Law of Defamation. Under this law it is usually a civil, but may if it is seditious, be a criminal offence, to make or publish in writing statements calculated to bring anyone into hatred, ridicule or contempt, or which cause the person to be ostracised. The law is technically divided into Slander, defamation by word or gesture, and, therefore, a temporary attack and Libel, defamation by the printed word, and, therefore, because it is recorded, a permanent attack.

A person cannot be restrained in advance from publishing something allegedly defamatory, but when it is published an action for damages and to restrain further publication can be made. Heavy damages have been awarded in some recent cases where a person's reputation has been seriously damaged, though a defence of 'fair comment' can be offered to protect the expression of opinion on a matter deemed to be a public interest.

d) Anything said or written which is neither seditious, blasphemous nor libellous, is acceptable provided that there is no breach of Race Relations legislation. Under the 1965 and 1968 acts, it was an offence to publicise views which may have the effect of provoking racial disharmony. By the 1976 one, the prosecution does not have to prove any intention to incite racial hatred, only that this was the consequence of what was said or done.

This is a good example of the law protecting some individuals at the expense of others. It is an inroad upon the right of free speech, but, arguably, is good for social harmony and necessary to safeguard the position of groups who feel threatened. In fact, prosecutions under this law have been rare and judges have leaned on the side of maximum free speech.

In one case, following the 1976 legislation, Judge McKinnon made himself controversial for his comments to the defendant after the jury found a National Front member not guilty of breaching the law. The accused was alleged to have made derogatory remarks about coloured people whom he described as 'racial interiors'. In addressing him, the Judge, in his zeal to see free speech protected, appeared to wish the man well with his future statements!

The limitations described in **a-d** are also relevant to what appears in THE PRESS, using the term to cover printed material of all types. Journalists have also to be wary in order not to offend against the Official Secrets Act of 1911, and in the prolonged Spycatcher case some papers were considerably limited as to what they were allowed to publish.

Journalists may also fall foul of the law by committing a contempt of court, by publishing comments in the course of a trial which might make it more difficult for justice to prevail. Similarly, early disclosure of reports by parliamentary committees could be a contempt of Parliament.

In the writing of books and magazines, the Obscene Publications Act is another possible pitfall. Most of the offences here have come into the so-called 'dirty books' category, though occasionally a work of alleged literary merit can become the centrepiece of a spectacular case (e.g. the 'Lady Chatterley' trial, 1959).

Thus, the attitude of English law towards freedom of discussion is that a speaker or writer has no special protection to give him free expression of his opinions, but that there is no restriction which can interfere with this freedom unless he over-steps the bounds set by law and, in particular, the law of defamation. The law throws the risk on the speaker, writer and publisher.

Of course 'the right of free speech is a perfectly separate thing from the question of the place where it is to be exercised.' (McAra v Magistrates of Edinburgh). Clearly, the exercise of the former depends upon a public place being available.

3. FREEDOM TO MARCH IN PROCESSION AND OF ASSEMBLY. It is traditional for British people to demonstrate their views on a political issue by marching in procession,

bearing placards about nuclear disarmament, unemployment or whatever issues arouse their particular interest. People may do this as the Queen's Highway is designed for travel from one place to another, and what an individual may do so may a number of individuals acting together. They have to be careful about stopping, which may be a wilful obstruction of the road network under the Highways Act of 1980, but if they keep moving in an orderly manner, this is legal.

The 1936 Public Order Act, passed because of Fascist disorders, gave the police power to change the route of a procession or impose conditions. In particular, it banned the carrying of weapons at public processions/meetings, and the wearing of uniforms.

It also gave a Chief Constable the right to apply to a local council for authority to prohibit processions for a period up to three months if the Home Secretary approves the application. In London, such permission is unnecessary and the Metropolitan Commissioner may himself make such an order, as in 1978 when the National Front were stopped from holding demonstrations because of concern that a breach of the peace might occur. The freedom of the NF to hold a rally may well conflict with the right of local residents (especially coloured ones) not to have provocative marchers passing by their front door.

In the last decade, a number of outbursts of violence (particularly those associated with demonstrations, industrial disputes, inner city riots and football hooliganism) revealed a need to update the law, and give the police stronger powers to avert public disorder.

Under the 1986 Public Order Act, some old offences have been removed, and new ones created. Those concerning racial hatred have been clarified and extended, exclusion orders in connection with football matches have been introduced, and the law on riot, violent disorder and affray has been substantially amended. Riot is the most serious of the offences in this area; where a minimum of twelve persons use or threaten unlawful violence, a person may be charged, and, if guilty, imprisoned for up to ten years.

4. FREEDOM OF MEETING TOGETHER. People may meet together in a public meeting if they can hire premises or meet on private property; they may also use a public park or shopping centre, if they have permission. On the public highway, they cannot commit obstruction unless they have police approval. The general principle governing public meetings is that people may say what they like provided it does not lead to a possible breakdown of public order.

Associated with freedom of expression and of association, is freedom of religion and public worship. Any religion or cult has the right to hold a service and practise its rituals freely, though dispute has occurred with a group such as Scientologists as to whether they are a religion, and whether their behaviour can be harmful and exploitative of its members. Similarly, the right not to practise any form of religion, indeed to be an avowed and outspoken atheist, is a basic one.

5. LEGAL RIGHTS. In addition to these related aspects of freedom of expression and association are a collection of legal rights. These include equality before the law, the right of all citizens whatever their gender, religion, race or background to be treated in the same way. For all people, the right of personal freedom is fundamental; everyone should be free to do and behave as they wish unless the law specially provides otherwise.

Magna Carta, in 1215, clearly stated that:

> *No freeman shall be taken or imprisoned or disseised (dispossessed) or exiled or in any way destroyed, nor will we go upon him nor will we send upon him except*

by the lawful judgement of his peers or (and) the law of the land.

The police have no general power to hold a person for questioning, but if they have reasonable grounds for thinking an offence has been committed, they may do so. If no arrest is made, they can ask a person to 'help them with their enquiries', an invitation difficult to refuse.

The citizen is protected from arbitrary arrest by the ancient writ of Habeas Corpus. Anyone who is detained for a 'serious arrestable offence' must be produced before a magistrates' court after 36 hours. Given the authorisation of the magistrates, detention can be continued for up to a maximum of 4 days. However, under the Prevention of Terrorism Acts, regularly renewed since 1975, a person can be held for up to a maximum of seven days without charge.

The right to a fair trial, the assumption that a person is presumed innocent until proven guilty and the right of the accused to silence, have been widely admired and accepted features of our legal system.

Social Rights

All of the rights so far referred to are civil and legal rights. It is markedly more difficult to be specific in the area of social rights, for here conflicting claims can be made; some alleged rights may conflict with others. The right of a woman to have total control over her own body (and thus have an abortion should she wish to do so) is not consistent with the right of the unborn foetus, a potential human being, to life. The freedom to picket in pursuance of an industrial dispute may conflict with the freedom of those who wish to work.

These are contentious matters and since the 1960s a number of measures in other controversial areas have introduced social rights offering greater protection for consumers, married women, racial minorities and homosexuals.

Many people would proffer the right to work as another basic one, but what if, perhaps as a result of government economic policy, no work is available? Others would speak of a right to health or education, but does that include the right to buy private treatment or schooling?

Similarly, the right to privacy is one increasingly claimed. Telephone tapping, industrial espionage, the storage of data such as credit records on computer, the keeping of medical and school files, all pose problems, and some countries have acknowledged the possible threat to privacy involved by recognising this right in law. In Britain, we have Data Protection legislation and controls on tapping.

In so many of the areas discussed, the difficulty is in balancing the competing claims of different individuals and groups; in striking a balance between the desire for personal liberty and the need for public security from unlawful behaviour, ranging from that of the petty criminal to the dangerous terrorist; and in granting maximum freedom to those of extremist views consistent with the preservation of a free society.

Chapter Two

Protection For Our Freedoms

In Britain, we have relied upon the rule of law for our protection, secure in the knowledge that the individual has the ultimate right of redress in the courts if an injustice has been done.

The citizen has a number of ways of seeking to influence the government and thereby of remedying wrongs done. His/her power to do so is the greater if a number of people feel the same way.

As to the remedies available, much depends upon the type of case under consideration. Where, for instance, an individual's property rights have been ignored - as in the Crichel Down case after World War Two - there may well have been maladministration and such a case might now go to the Parliamentary Commissioner for Administration (Ombudsman). Where a Department's discretion has been involved, such as in the payment of social security benefits, or where a person has wrongfully been dismissed from work, an administrative tribunal could be the answer.

More specifically in the areas of civil and legal rights, the citizen may well employ a number of approaches before a case ever reaches the courts. Writing to newspapers, gaining the attention of the media, lobbying an MP, working via a pressure group such as Liberty, or engaging in demonstrations and forms of direct action, have all been employed. An active, effective MP who uses opportunities within the House and via the media can be useful; much more so is the backing of other MPs, maybe the opposition or preferably back benchers on the government side. Yet in any appeal to Parliament, political considerations are likely to be a significant factor affecting the outcome.

In many cases, individuals and groups have exhausted such opportunities, maybe even gone through the courts to gain redress. At the end of the day, they may have still felt that their rights have not been recognised and protected. In some cases redress has only finally been achieved by a 'European' solution.

This usually involves the Court in Strasbourg, which enforces the European Convention on Human Rights, of which more later. However EC law reflects much of the spirit of the Convention, and decisions of the European Court of Justice in Luxembourg have in recent years covered such areas as the right of workers, and particularly of women.

As a result of its judgements, Jackie Drake gained an Invalid Care Allowance previously only available to men and single women, and Helen Marshall, a dietician in the NHS won the right to work on until 65 as men already did. In both cases, the British Government had to back down and bring in legislation complying with Community Law for this trumps any British statute.

A direct approach to the Luxembourg Court by a private individual is very unusual and expensive. Citizens can, however, defend their interests by approaching the EC Commission or the European Parliament. Petitions submitted have covered topics ranging from the unequal treatment of men and women to entitlements to pensions and social security, and satisfactory redress has sometimes been brought about in such cases which usually concern people who travel frequently within the Community on business.

Such developments show that the 'European' solution is one of increasing importance; it can be employed, but it is not able to provide speedy justice under current arrangements.

These means of gaining redress may well work in particular circumstances, but it is often argued that, given some of the developments of recent years, our freedoms need a more certain protection than is now available.

The Threat to Freedom

It is often said that the threat to our liberties is not a dramatic, but rather an insidious one. Rights traditionally acknowledged may be whittled away, the danger coming from many sources. The increasing concentration of power in Whitehall, the growth in the extent and complexity of government work, the strength of the government's position in the House of Commons, the growing mood of intolerance towards minority groups (be they racial or homosexual), are all cited as evidence of the need for some more substantial protection for our rights.

Although in recent years, Parliament has granted extra rights to some groups, on other occasions it has acted illiberally. Armed with its majority, the government of the day pushed through legislation which, whatever its justification, jeopardised people's rights. The difficulties of the Northern Ireland situation have led to a series of measures which breach the rule of law. Internment in 1972, trial without jury in the Diplock courts, the successive

Prevention of Terrorism Acts and, more recently, the limitations imposed on the media in its coverage of the IRA and the changes concerning the right to silence, all involve a serious curtailment of individual rights.

Chapter Three

Support for a British Bill of Rights

It was in the late 1960s that we first began to hear calls for a Bill of Rights. They came from groups and individuals across the political spectrum, extending from Fabians on the Left, to the Liberals in the Centre and, most notably, to Quintin Hogg on the Right, in his 'New Charter' publication.

The House of Commons examined bills and the Lords debated 'the need for protection of human rights and fundamental freedoms' in 1969. By the mid-'70s, the topic had entered the realms of serious political debate, especially when, in the 1974 Hamlyn lecture, (the now) Lord Scarman took up the theme, as

19

did Lord Hailsham in his 1976 Dimbleby lecture. Having become ennobled, Quintin Hogg was now arguing for a written constitution as well as a Bill of Rights.

Their views have subsequently provoked much constitutional discussion in journals and in Parliament. Some academics, a number of eminent lawyers and judges, as well as several politicians, have leant their support. Generally speaking, in the last few years MPs and writers representing the Centre-Left in British politics have been the most active enthusiasts for a Bill, believing that we should forestall any danger of our rights being eroded or whittled away. In the words of Paddy Ashdown, the Liberal Leader, 'a Bill of Rights is an essential, guaranteed and constitutional buttress for individual freedom, particularly in our centralised and unrepresentative political system'. The official Labour Party has not in the past offered any significant support for such a measure, whatever its anxieties about a threat to freedom in Thatcherite Britain. John Smith's leadership has, however, seen a departure from the traditional Labour outlook.

Significantly, some of the voices on the Right put forward their case at a time when there was a Labour Government after 1974. The October election had yielded a government with a bare parliamentary majority (soon reduced), elected by under 30% of the total electorate. The Government proceeded to seek to pass measures which were controversial, for instance concerning nationalisation, race relations and the closed shop, on the basis that such policies had been in their manifesto. Faced by the prospect of Labour governments, even minority ones, introducing 'drastic' measures which might be difficult to reverse, a Bill of Rights seemed particularly attractive. A decade of Conservative rule has removed many of the fears of writers and thinkers on the political Right.

There is certainly no consensus as to whether we need a Bill of Rights, but even among those who favour one the motives which give rise to their support differ significantly. On the Left, the issue is seen more in terms of civil liberties which are sometimes overridden, especially those of minority groups. On the Right, there has been a tendency to emphasise what they see as the creeping advance of the socialist bureaucratic state in which individual rights can be ignored by such things as compulsory purchase orders and measures of public ownership.

Thus in practice, for a group of eminent lawyers and politicians to sit down, charged with the task of devising a bill, is no guarantee that one would emerge. There would be agreement that some rights were fundamental like the right to life, liberty, personal security, and freedom of speech and association, but the liberty of an individual or group often has to be weighed against other political and social values.

On the so-called social rights, there would be some disagreement. The Right-inclined members would perhaps wish to stress the property rights threatened by socialist measures; the Left might stress rights of union membership, peaceful picketing and strike action.

Again, some persons, especially perhaps of third parties, might feel that in listing democratic rights, apart from the right of all adults to vote in free elections, they would like to see a commitment to 'fair voting'. Others might favour a Freedom of Information Act and a generally more open system of government.

In other words, to devise a Bill satisfactory to all those interested in the subject and acceptable to the rest of the population, might be highly complex. It might have to be vague or too weak to command widespread support.

The European Convention?

Many of the difficulties in drafting our own statement would be overcome if we opted to incorporate the European Convention into our own system of law, for most supporters of a Bill of Rights, be they of either political persuasion or none, can accept the substance of it. Having been ratified by a Labour government, and accepted and renewed by Conservative ones, it has the considerable advantage of being acceptable, in varying degrees of enthusiasm, to both political wings.

Chapter Four

The European Convention on Human Rights

The Council of Europe believed that fundamental freedoms were best upheld by countries which were effective political democracies with a 'common heritage of political traditions, ideals, freedom and the rule of law'. In November 1950, Ministers of 15 member countries signed the European Convention on Human Rights and it came into force on 3.9.1953. All 28 present members of the Council have signed; some have incorporated the Convention into their own legal system, but where this has not happened a country's law should not conflict with it.

Table 1: Signatories of the Convention

Austria	Liechtenstein
Belgium	Luxembourg
Bulgaria	Malta
Cyrus	Netherlands
Czech Republic	Norway
Denmark	Poland
Finland	Portugal
France	San Marino
Germany	Slovakia
Greece	Spain
Hungary	Sweden
Iceland	Switzerland
Ireland	Turkey
Italy	United Kingdom

These figures and others in Chapters Four and Five relate to the period to January 1. 1993 Since then, four nations have joined the Council, but have yet to ratify the Convention. Many more states are keen to join.

In the 40 years after 1953, 10 new rights and obligations have been added in what are known as the Protocols, and states can choose which they wish to accept. The important ninth one has yet to come into force; this allows individuals to refer a case to the Court, directly. A tenth is now 'open to signature'.

Since the Convention came into force, any state has been able to complain to the Commission that another signatory state has failed to comply with it. Moreover, in addition, all signatories have accepted that individual applications may be made from citizens in a country who wish to complain about treatment they have received from their government (Article 25). Most of the Commission's work concerns such individual applications.

Contents of the European Convention

There are 66 Articles in the Convention and some of these are listed in the document on pp 26-27, published by the Council of Europe. The terms used, such as freedom of peaceful assembly

24

and association' are broad; this can be viewed either as desirable or as a disadvantage. If the wording was more precise, it could be more difficult to place a grievance within the terminology used; looser, all-embracing phraseology offers much more scope when presenting a case. On the other hand, vague phrases require interpretation as to whether they are applicable in individual circumstances, and such judgements ultimately will be made not by elected politicians but by unaccountable judges.

Procedure

Members of any state wishing to use the right of individual petition (under Article 25) first contact the European Commission. They must do this within six months of a final decision by the authorities within their country, having exhausted all of the other opportunities to gain redress. More than 5000 letters are received each year by the Commission of which around 1/3 are deemed to qualify for an examination of their admissibility.

An initial survey is made in which the relevant government and the applicant may be contacted for factual information, and the applicant is usually legally represented; if necessary, legal aid is available to those of limited means. The Commission then decides if the application is admissible (altogether, more than 20,000 cases have been registered as such) and if it is, it proceeds to examine the complaint in depth, establishing the facts of the case from all parties concerned.

It tries to act as a mediator, seeking a friendly settlement, but if one is not reached, the Commission draws up a detailed report. These reports present all the facts and offer a legal opinion as to whether there is a breach of the Convention. A copy is sent to the appropriate government for it to consider and to the Committee of Ministers, the decision-making body of the Council of Europe. The document is confidential at this stage, its contents unknown to the applicant.

Table 2: The European Convention on Human Rights:

Every Member of the Council of Europe must accept the principles of the rule of law and of the enjoyment by all persons within its jurisdiction of human rights and fundamental freedoms.

Articles 3 of the Statute of the Council of Europe, London, 5 May 1949.

Fundamental freedoms which are the foundation of justice and peace in the world ... are best maintained on the one hand by an effective political democracy and on the other by a common understanding and observance of the human rights upon which they depend.

Preamble to the European Convention on Human Rights, Rome, 4 November 1950.

The Rights Protected

Most of the rights and freedoms protected by the Convention and its protocols are of a civil and political nature. The main ones are:

- the right to life, to liberty and security of person and to a fair trial.

- respect for private and family life, home and correspondence.

- freedom of thought, conscience and religion.

- freedom of expression (including freedom of the press).

- freedom of peaceful assembly and association, including the right to join a trade union.

- the right to have a sentence reviewed by a higher tribunal.

- the right to marry and found a family.

- the equality of rights and responsibilities of spouses during marriage.

- the right to peaceful enjoyment of possessions.

- the right to education.

- certain rights concerning elections.

- liberty of movement and freedom to choose where to live.

- the right to leave a country including one's own.

Further rights stem from the prohibition of:

- criminal laws that are retroactive.

- torture and inhuman or degrading treatment or punishment

- the death penalty (Protocol 6).

- slavery, servitude and forced labour.

- discrimination in the enjoyment of rights and freedoms guaranteed by the Convention.

- expulsion of a state's own nationals or denying them entry.

The Convention sensibly recognises that most of these rights cannot be unlimited in a democratic society and that restrictions may be necessary on grounds of public safety or national security, to protect the economic wellbeing of a country, public health and morals or the rights and freedoms of others, or to prevent disorder and crime. It also permits states, on certain conditions, to suspend their obligations in time of war or other public emergency. But no state can avoid its obligation to respect the right to life and the bans on torture, the death penalty, slavery and the retroactivity of the criminal law.

This extract and other tables in the Chapter are taken from 'The Council of Europe and the Protection of Human Rights,' December 1992 (Published on behalf of the Council of Europe, and freely available from it).

Table 3: Examples of Cases

Individual complaints which have been referred to the Court cover an ever-increasing range of issues.

- Notable examples of these are:
- right of access to the courts
- length of legal proceedings
- various aspects of detention (mental patients, terrorist suspects, vagrants)
- criminal proceedings in the absence of the accused
- use of corporal punishment (in schools, or as a judicial punishment)
- prisoners' rights
- control of telephone 'tapping' and surveillance of correspondence.
- laws on homosexual activities
- social security disputes (health insurance, industrial accidents)
- status of illegitimate children
- trade union activities, including the 'closed shop'
- immigration and deportation regulations
- status of transsexuals
- freedom of expression, including restrictions on press reporting
- compulsory sex education in schools
- property rights.

Inter-state applications brought before the Commission by one member state against another have involved, amongst other things, the situation in Greece under the Colonels' regime, methods of interrogating terrorist suspects in Northern Ireland (the only inter-state case so far referred to the Court), the consequences of Turkish military action in Cyprus and the situation in Turkey between 1980 and 1982.

Within three months of the report being issued the case may go to the European Court. The country must have accepted its compulsory jurisdiction, but all have now done this. The referral can be made by the Commission or government, not by the individual concerned. If the case is not submitted to the Court, the Committee of Ministers makes a ruling (on a majority basis) as to whether the Convention has been infringed. As with the Court's decisions, those of the Committee of Ministers are final and binding.

The European Court

The Court adjudicates on all contentious matters concerning the interpretation of the Convention. To consider a case, 7 judges (including the one representing the state concerned) meet and after consideration of the evidence give their verdict on a majority vote. This judgement is binding on the member states.

Of the 368 judgements delivered by the Court since its creation in 1959, in 231 it has been found that there has been a violation of the Convention; when this is so, the Court can provide for 'just satisfaction' (compensation) to be paid to the injured party, and has done so in the majority of cases. A protocol of 1970 also allows the Court to offer an advisory opinion on a particular issue, but this has yet to be employed.

Table 4: The Work of the Court

	New Referrals to Court	Judgements of the Court
1959	0	0
1960	2	1
1969	2	2
1979	3	5
1987	21	32
1988	16	26
1989	31	25
1990	61	30
1991	93	72
1992	50	81

Changes in the Machinery?

In recent years, the existence of the Convention has become more widely known; in the last two years alone, (1991, 1992) 11425 Provisional Files were opened by the Commission, and 3479 were examined for registration as to their 'admissibility'. Not surprisingly, given the increase in its workload, delays in the procedure are serious and it can take six years to get a Court verdict; on one occasion it took 16 years. This increased burden reflects an increase in public awareness of the machinery and its success in eventually producing a worthwhile verdict, rather than a horrendous increase in the number of violations of basic rights. The Court itself now gives many rulings a year compared to one per annum in its first decade, as the figures in Table 4 illustrate.

Whereas it took the Court 26 years to 'notch up' its first 100 judgements, the next 100 were delivered in only 4. In 1990, the President of the Court was moved to speak of a situation where the machinery 'will no longer be able to operate in the way it does at present'. Protocol Nine, allowing direct access to the Court where the Commission has declared a case as 'admissible', could aggravate the burden, for some less important cases might now consume its valuable time; if they were serious applications, they have in the past reached the Court anyway.

To expedite the machinery, countries were urged to sign Protocol 8, which was aimed at speeding up proceedings before the Commission. It has now come into operation, and allows Chambers of only seven members (or in some cases, Committees of three) to look at less difficult cases. Two Chambers and six Committees have been set up, and the Commission's capacity to meet its extra work-load has therefore been considerably increased.

Other possibilities were considered over a long period. These included a reduction in the supervisory duties of the Committee of Ministers or even a merger of the Commission and the Court. A new building in Strasbourg, designed to house all the human rights machinery, was provided to enable better staffing and more deliberation rooms; work has begun on this.

Table 5: How the Human Rights Institutions Work

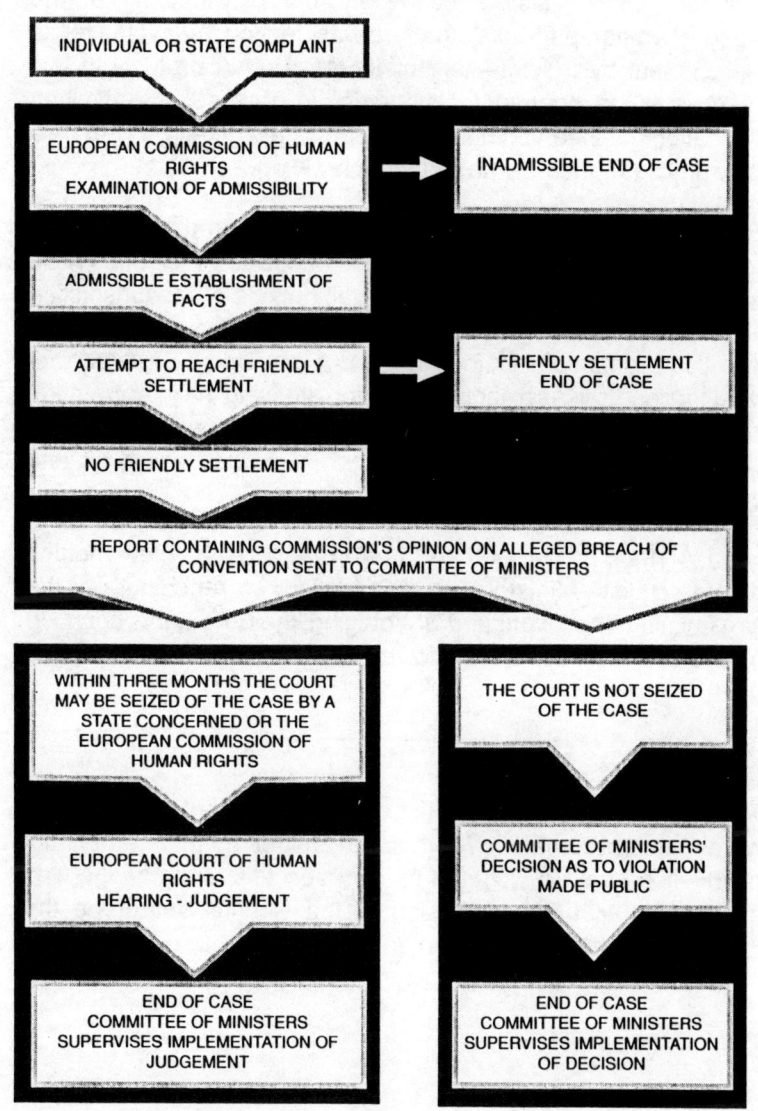

New Arrangements

For ten years, Britain was viewed as obstructive by other members because it blocked proposals for much-needed reform. In October 1993, Ministers conceded that restructuring of the present two-tier, part-time structure was needed, and voted for its replacement by a single-tier, full-time Court. A protocol to this effect is to be opened for signature in May 1994 and when ratification has been completed by each state (itself likely to be a slow process), the new arrangements will apply.

Each state will, as now, have a single judge on the Court, and committees of three will screen cases to decide which ones raise issues already resolved and which fall outside of the jurisdiction of the machinery. Chambers of seven judges will normally adjudicate on issues before the Court, but Britain insisted that where a case 'raises a serious question affecting the interpretation or application of the Convention' then, in these exceptional circumstances, a 'grand chamber' of 17 judges would sit and decide.

In early 1994, having agreed to reform proposals a few months before, British Ministers were accused of reneging on the streamlining endeavour and 'sabotaging' the Euro-rights court. In a renewed attempt to slow down progress, Britain was isolated 31-1.

The old process was a product of its time, an era when states were reluctant to hand over their sovereignty to an international court. It became a victim of its own success, and change was needed for with the expansion of the Council of Europe the case-load is set to increase even more.

Chapter Five

Britain and The European Convention

Britain was the first country to ratify the Convention in 1951. A Labour Government gave British citizens the right to complain to the Commission in Strasbourg in 1965 and this right of individual petition has been subsequently renewed five yearly, latterly in January 1991.

The record of British governments at Strasbourg has been unimpressive for few other member countries have had more individual cases referred to it (currently approaching 1000 a year), have had as many declared admissible by the Commission or have fared so badly in the European Court. Out of 49 cases which had been adjudicated upon by the Court, 30 have been lost by successive governments, and in many of them compensation was laid down as payable to the aggrieved citizen. Until 1990, the overall British record was far worse than that of any other country, but the Italians and the French have frequently fallen foul of the Convention in the last couple of years.

Table 6: Countries with the Worst Record at Strasbourg Since 1986
a. The Commission

Country	No. of Provisional Files							No. of Cases Registered to test if they are 'Admissible'						
	1986	1987	1988	1989	1990	1991	1992	1986	1987	1988	1989	1990	1991	1992
France	381	513	560	714	1017	1728	1648	86	115	139	212	248	400	353
Italy	200	369	599	667	353	463	471	62	110	171	142	154	133	196
Sweden	180	198	208	223	247	225	233	68	77	88	84	125	90	82
United Kingdom	763	781	768	925	1067	843	908	38	140	145	224	236	202	222
(West) Germany	539	522	606	717	618	620	601	106	108	113	169	147	139	137

b. Total Number of Court Judgements Involving at Least One Violation.

Country	Number of cases
Austria	22
Belgium	19
France	16
Germany	10
Italy	70
Netherlands	15
Sweden	18
Switzerland	12
United Kingdom	30

Among the cases in which the British government has been involved have been allegations of ill-treatment in Northern Ireland (the Maze prison), judicial birching in the Isle of Man, restrictions on a prisoner's right to respect for correspondence, corporal punishment in state schools in Scotland and in private schools in England, and the dismissal of British railwaymen following an agreement making membership of trade union a condition of employment. In the latter case in 1981, after three men (Young, Webster and James) had petitioned Strasbourg, £46,215 was awarded in compensation.

Of the cases currently before the Commission, amongst the many involving the United Kingdom, several concern the denial of legal aid when a prisoner is appealing against conviction and sentence, and some others relate to problems of children in care. Specific ones include the following;

- The right to engage in sado-masochistic practices in private.

- The refusal to recognise a change of sex, in law.

- The refusal to release an Aids sufferer on compassionate grounds

- The length of time taken by the Parole Board to review a discretionary life-sentence.

Early in 1994 it was announced that Hugo Greenhalge and his gay friend were going to the European Court after the Commission ruled that their case was 'admissible'. They believed that the new age of consent for homosexuals (18) is in breach of two articles on privacy and discrimination against minorities. If the Court eventually rules in their favour - the case may take two or three years - then the Government could be forced to change its legislation. The two men want to see the age of consent equalised at 16 for gays and heterosexuals.

Case Study One

One of the most well-publicised judgements passed by the European Court involving Britain was proclaimed on 29.11.88. Yet again, the British Government was found to be guilty of a breach of human rights. Four men, Terence Brogan, Dermot Coyle, William McFadden and Michael Tracey were held under the 1984 Prevention of Terrorism Act for periods ranging from 4 days and 6 hours to 6 days and 17 hours, and then released without charge. Under the Act, detainees could be held for 48 hours, but the Secretary of State for Northern Ireland had the power to authorise an extension for up to a maximum of 5 further days.

The European Court ruled by 12 votes to 7 that their experience fell foul of the requirement that anyone arrested for terrorist offences must be taken 'promptly' before the court. Even the shortest period of detention breached 'the strict constraints of the time permitted by the notion of promptness'. The PTA failed to give suspects the right to a 'prompt appearance before a judicial authority', a breach of Article 5 (3) of the Convention.

The four persons involved decided to seek substantial compensation from the government and as this could not be amicably agreed their lawyer went to Strasbourg to have an amount laid down. No compensation was awarded, the finding of a violation being considered to constitute 'just satisfaction'.

For the Government, which at the time had just published its new Prevention of Terrorism Bill, there was a difficult decision to make in the light of the rulings. Ministers examined ways of circumnavigating the decision and had three options. They could reduce the maximum 7 days period perhaps to a maximum of 4, as many Labour and Democrat MPs wanted; given the difficult circumstances of terrorist activity in Northern Ireland, this may have been acceptable to the court. Secondly, they could seek a 'derogation of non-compliance' on the grounds that compliance would jeopardise national security. Thirdly, they could establish a tribunal which would decide whether a further detention after 48 hours was justified. This would give the stamp of judicial approval to seven day detentions. Fundamentally, it was not the length of detentions which worried the Court but the lack of judicial scrutiny. The Court does not specify a particular type of control.

So that it had time to examine the topic further and perhaps work out the detail of any tribunal scheme, the Government initially issued a derogation, the escape clause in Article 15. This was drafted to meet emergency situations 'threatening the life of the nation' such as war. However tragic the Irish situation is, whatever the cost to victims and their relatives, this was seen by many observers as a generous interpretation of the terms of the clause. The Government itself has usually portrayed terrorism as a threat rather than as a national emergency. Between 1971 and 1984, the UK did use derogation powers to protect its emergency provisions, but after that 'special powers' replaced 'emergency procedures', and derogation was lifted. Since the Court's ruling, no changes have been made in the PTA machinery, and the derogation has been renewed.

In the past, in cases where the Court has ruled against Britain, governments have usually complied. The Conservatives place much emphasis on the rule of law and during the European proceedings the Government never gave any indication that it would fail to comply with the ultimate ruling. Some backbenchers on the Tory Right wanted the Home Secretary to defy the Court, and would have been happy if Britain withdrew from its jurisdiction.

However, in May 1993, the Court gave its judgement on a review of the derogation procedure in this case. The finding assuaged any Tory anxieties, for it was accepted that it was legitimate for the Government to describe the situation as an emergency, and that the derogation lodged by the UK satisfies the requirements of Article 15.

Case Study Two

In 1983, a 15 year old boy was caned by his Headmaster (four strokes throught the trousers) for defacing the cover of another pupil's file. His mother took him to a GP who diagnosed heavy bruising and swelling of the buttocks. The police initially advised that there was evidence of actual bodily harm, but later decided not to proceed. A civil action for assault was dismissed by the County Court jugde, for he argued that the parents' contract with the school allowed caning. (The incident occurred before caning was banned in British State and publically-funded independent schools in 1987, after a series of applications to Strasbourg).

In this case, resolved in 1992, the man (whose identity was not revealed) received £8000 in compensation after the Commission decided that the punishment amounted to degrading treatment, in breach of the Convention. The issue of caning in schools provides a good example of how British governments have been forced to modify their approach in the light of several European rulings.

The Situation in 1994

Having agreed to proposals to reform the Strasbourg machinery, Britain appeared to be slowing down the implementation of these decisions. Within the 32-member Council of Europe, it argued against an unconditional right of individual petition. The Home Secretary, Michael Howard, was understood to be unenthusiastic about Article 25, and was keen to ensure that the right of five-yearly review was retained. Other countries wanted to see the right made permanent in all member-states, a move which it was felt would be a good example to the new Eastern European democracies which needed to demonstrate their attachments to human rights.

Yet again, the British Government seemed to be barely committed to reforms in the European machinery, a reflection perhaps of the Whitehall view which has always seen the Commission and Court as an irritating inconvenience.

Chapter Six

The Case For a Bill Of Rights

The benefits of a Bill are said to be many and varied. They range from the need to keep Parliament on its toes to protecting basic civil liberties from ensuring that laws passed do not neglect such concerns to the need to prevent a humiliating rush by British citizens to the European Court because at home they have no code of practice to which they can appeal. Above all, a Bill would re-emphasize the right of individuals against the state, rights which are always in danger of erosion.

Advocates on the Left speak more of the threat to civil liberties which are sometimes overridden by public bodies such as the Civil Service and the police. In several cases, Liberal/Labour writers have emphasised how the rights of particular minority groups have been infringed. In 1968, Kenyan Asians who held British passports were deprived of their rights of citizenship in Great Britain, when controls were placed on their entry - by a Labour Government! In 1984, trade unionists at GCHQ were asked to renounce their union membership because of the alleged security problems which industrial action could cause there; this case was investigated by the European Commission.

Supporters on the Right tend to emphasise the dangers of a steady extension of the socialist state in periods of Labour government. Individual rights can be overridden by such things as excessive trade union power (e.g. closed shop agreements) or the attempted removal of pay beds from the NHS.

From either political standpoint and none, there are those who are keen to see us have some statements of rights which can be quoted by any group or citizen who feel their rights are being ignored or trampled upon. The phrases of such statements are deliberately expressed in broad terms such as the 'right to liberty and security of the person' and the 'right to freedom of thought'. It is up to a judge to decide whether there has been a breach of such wide terms.

The possibility of forcing the government to defend its position in a court of law considerably enhances the power of the individual. The government would have to view any complaint brought against it seriously, and if no defence was offered then the judge would automatically adjudicate against the relevant department.

The Case for the European Convention

If we enact the European Convention into British law, as all but five other member states of the Council have done, this would do away with the problems of devising a Bill of our own. As such statements go it is generally thought to be fairly drafted and, broad though its provisions inevitably are, supporters believe that it would afford greater protection for our civil liberties than that offered in British law at present. It has now survived for some 40 yeas and no major flaws have yet become apparent.

Declaratory statements of rights have to avoid being either so vague that they are meaningless or so detailed that they can become a regular political battlefield. This one steers a course between extremes. Of course, it won't please everyone on either side of the political divide. Some of its provisions such as those on education are likely to be unattractive to Labour just as many Conservatives would perhaps be uneasy about clauses relating to rights of assembly and association. Yet whatever sacrifices would have to be made, the benefits outweigh the costs involved, especially at a time when the rights of the individual are under constant assault. Individuals would have a clearer idea of their rights and would have definite backing in their bid to stop governmental infringements of them.

To incorporate the Convention would remove any uncertainties about its status in British law. Our ratification of it has, of course, ultimately imposed obligations upon us already, but at present the position is something of a constitutional absurdity. The courts in Britain are not bound by its provisions, nor is it part of British law; it cannot be employed by the citizen wishing to sue a government department such as the Home Office. Yet its terms are binding upon the government for if the European Court decides against us then ministers must promise to change the law; they may also have to pay compensation.

Swifter justice, a more speedy protection for our rights, would be available if our courts could apply the Convention in their judgements. Appealing to the European Commission is necessarily a ponderous procedure often taking five or six years; it also involves revealing our 'dirty washing' in an international arena for all to see. Incorporating the Convention would enable us to fulfil our obligations for currently we have signed it but not made it part of British law. Article 13 is clear in its requirements. 'Everyone whose rights and freedoms as set forth in this Convention are violated shall have an effective remedy before a national authority'. If a national authority (in the form of our courts) was to be made available to British citizens, then judges would have a useful body of accumulated European case law to assist them in making their judgements.

Governments would no longer be able to 'play for time', knowing that it is several years before the European machinery reaches a final decision. Departments which know that they are ultimately likely to lose a case, are currently tempted to fight to the bitter end before they rectify an abuse, secure in the knowledge that by the time of the verdict much of the political controversy will have died away. The whole dilatory procedure would be short-cut if British courts enforce the Convention in their own right.

A Bill of Rights is not a panacea for all of our ills, but its advocates see it as a way of offering some protection against the abuse of power. If the slow and expensive process of 'going to Strasbourg' could be replaced by a relatively quick settlement in our native courts, then not only would there be a legal restraint upon infringements of personal rights, but also a moral one. Any government would be more hesitant in passing legislation which could contravene the spirit of a Bill of Rights, and such a measure might well educate administrators and lawyers, politicians and judges to be more vigilant in safeguarding personal liberties.

Chapter Seven

The Case Against a Bill of Rights

Official Party Attitudes.

The official Conservative Party has shown little interest in any suggestions of a British Bill of Rights, and even those erstwhile supporters such as Lord Hailsham have been notably silent on the subject since the party regained office in 1979. His worries about an 'elective dictatorship' were significantly greater at a time of Labour government in the mid-late '70s. Some MPs have been interested in incorporating the European Convention into British law, but as yet John Major, like his predecessor, is unconvinced of the case for change.

The Labour Party, which might be expected to be more concerned about measures to provide greater respect for minority rights, has in the past shown a notable lack of sympathy for this particular constitutional reform. The Policy Review group meeting after the 1987 election defeat was concerned with other ways of promoting individual rights.

The general view in the party has been that not only is such a measure unnecessary - as our rights are better protected in Parliament, via MPs - but that it wouldn't work anyway, as a means of securing basic liberties. The fear is that such a bill could actually stifle libertarian and progressive legislation.

Politicians on the Left, sceptical of a Bill of Rights, may have noted how the comment of Lord Hailsham a decade or so ago illustrated their fears; 'the present Government ... is persistently proposing legislation ... which would almost certainly be caught' by such a Bill. His thoughts and those of like-minded thinkers were directed towards dreaming up any measures which would place a check on the unbridled power of a small parliamentary majority such as the Labour Government then had. They might hope to stop an extension of nationalisation and any other socialist measures they wishes to thwart.

Labour has traditionally seen a Bill of Rights as representing a negative approach to freedom, and claimed that governmental action to promote equality before the law, to give minorities positive rights and to create a more open system of administration, was the best way forward. It saw this as a more convincing way of ensuring that those who have least and suffer discrimination achieve greater justice.

If we incorporated the Convention, a Labour Government might find Article 2 of the 1st Protocol troublesome, for though it asserts 'the right to education' it also refers to the 'right of parents to ensure that such education and teaching are in conformity with their own religious and philosophical convictions'. This has been interpreted by some writers as a barrier to the abolition of private schools. A clause such as Article 5, permitting 'the detention ... of persons of unsound mind, alcoholics or drug addicts or vagrants', people who may not have committed a specific offence, could also be obnoxious to some libertarians.

Fears concerning the Judiciary

In addition to doubts about the motives of some of those who want a Bill and anxieties about exactly what it might say, opponents have suspicion about those who would adjudicate on whether any violation of rights had occurred. Traditional Labour fears about the judiciary are highly relevant, for the Left has long held the view that judges veer towards protecting property rights rather than the interests of the whole community.

Their family background and education are said to incline them to a conservative viewpoint, for they often come from wealthy, professional upper middle-classes, having been educated at public school and Oxbridge. Moreover, they often reach their eminence at a fairly advanced age. Like so many people in 'top' positions in public life, in institutions ranging from the higher civil service to the church, they are very unrepresentative of the people.

Such a privileged background doesn't, of course, necessarily mean that they must be biased but some on the Left would argue that an innate caution, a preference for traditional standards of behaviour, respect for family and property, an emphasis on the maintenance of order, a distaste for minorities (particularly strident ones), are part of the training they receive.

The Labour movement, especially its trade union wing, has on occasions, fared badly in the courts, particularly in matters of industrial relations. Most famously in the Taff Vale dispute at the turn of the century, or more recently in some of the sequestration cases, verdicts have been very damaging to the union cause, and a suspicion of judges is therefore deep-rooted on the Left. These would be very people to arbitrate on what was or was not unconstitutional behaviour.

Several opponents, not just those on the Left, believe that there could be a further politicisation of the judiciary, for judges would be brought directly into the political arena in deciding whether governmental legislation was valid. As Lord Lloyd put it: 'To try to bring the judiciary into this sort of contest can only have one effect and that is to destroy the standing of the judiciary in the eyes of the people as a whole'.

The Sovereignty of Parliament

Clearly, judges would have to decide more issues of policy for the vague phrases of the European Convention, such as 'respect for private family life, home and correspondence' would have to be applied to individual cases and their meaning amplified. To many critics, it should be elected and accountable politicians who take policy decisions and resolve any conflicts of social and political values, for the sovereignty of Parliament (see pp 55-56) is often portrayed as a key principle of our democracy. Such decisions are political rather than judicial.

A More Positive Approach to Rights

If, opponents say, we feel that Parliament can no longer protect our rights then this is a reason for measures being taken to make it more effective, such as giving backbenchers more opportunity to acquire greater influence and control over the government. The rights needing protection are either already secure, or, if this is not the case, can be protected though parliamentary action. This might include measures to make our system of government more open, such as reform of the Official Secrets legislation and a Freedom of Information Act. Police powers of arrest and interrogation, the Prevention of Terrorism Act, the holding of large numbers of prisoners on remand - all are areas where reform might help promote a more liberal society in which rights are acknowledged, whereas a Bill of Rights could, in some respect, retard social advance.

Doubts about the Contents of a Bill

Finally, there is anxiety about the contents of any list of rights. Whilst few would quarrel with concepts such as the right to life, liberty, the ownership of property and peaceful assembly in the abstract, the difficulty occurs when we try and apply them to particular circumstances. Rights are not in most cases absolute and their relevance can very with the prevailing social and political climate; one person's right to liberty can conflict with the general needs of society. Social progress for the majority usually involves a diminution of someone's rights.

When speaking of one particular freedom, the Right and Left can interpret the topic very differently. By economic freedom, Labour might think in terms of freedom from poverty and unemployment, problems requiring state action to remedy them. To a Conservative, economic freedom means precisely the opposite; freedom from state interference, liberating the individual's initiative and allowing a person to do as seems in his/her best interests.

There is certainly no ready agreement on which rights are basic ones. When governments legislate in the social and economic field, their policies inevitably infringe the rights of someone; other parties portray these violations as heinous and unacceptable. One side emphasises one set of rights as fundamental - these may be sharply contested by the other side. Some of the rights claimed may be in conflict with other ones. This absence of agreement explains why a new Bill of Rights would be hard to draw up and even the broad terms of the European Convention do not provide a cause around which Left and Right could rally.

Chapter Eight

Overseas Experience

Many countries give their citizens a formal guarantee of their basic freedoms. Often, this is part of a larger constitutional settlement involving a written constitution.

United States of America

The American Revolutionaries who won independence for their country were much influenced by contemporary writers and political theorists. Their Declaration of Independence (1776) provided the rationale for the revolution, and a set of principles which would form the basis of the new nation being created;

We hold these truths to be self-evident. That all men are created equal, that they are endowed by their Creator with certain inalienable rights ... that to secure these rights governments are instituted among men, deriving their just Powers from the consent of the governed.

These beliefs were to represent the underlying values of the Constitution and Bill of Rights, in their emphasis upon political and legal equality. The Constitution was drawn up in 1787 and finally ratified two years later. However, whereas the framers of the document took the view that if rights were inborn and inalienable then a statement enumerating them was unnecessary, their opponents felt that a clear listing of them was essential. It would be beneficial to the people, a restraining influence upon rulers and a basis for any future court judgements.

To satisfy such a feeling, Congress passed ten amendments to the Constitution in 1791 and these are collectively known as the Bill of Rights. They laid down civil, religious and legal rights which are protection against invasion from congressional legislation, and can be seen below and on the following page.

Table 7: The US Bill Of Rights

Article I - Congress shall make no law respecting an establishment of religion, or prohibiting the free exercise thereof; or abridging the freedom of speech, or of the press; or the right of the people peaceably to assemble, and to petition the Government for a redress of grievances.

Article II - A well regulated Militia, being necessary to the security of a free State, the right of the people to keep and bear Arms, shall not be infringed.

Article III - No Soldier shall, in time of peace be quartered in any house, without the consent of the Owner, nor in time of war, but in a manner to be prescribed by law.

Article IV - The right of the people to be secure in their persons, houses, papers, and effects, against unreasonable searches and seizures, shall not be violated, and no Warrants shall issue, but upon probable cause, supported by Oath or affirmation, and particularly describing the place to be searched, and the persons or things to be seized.

Article V - No person shall be held to answer for a capital, or otherwise infamous crime, unless on a presentment or indictment of a Grand Jury, except in cases arising in the land or naval forces, or in the Militia, when in actual service in time of War or public danger; nor shall any person be subject for the same offence to be twice put in jeopardy of life or limb; nor shall be compelled in any criminal case to be a witness against himself, nor be deprived of life, liberty, or property, without due process of law; nor shall private property be taken for public use, without just compensation.

Article VI - In all criminal prosecutions, the accused shall enjoy the right to a speedy and public trial, by an impartial jury of the State and district wherein the crime shall have been committed, which district shall have been previously ascertained by law, and to be informed of the nature and cause of the accusation; to be confronted with the witnesses against him; to have compulsory process for obtaining witnesses in his favor, and to have the assistance of Counsel for his defence.

Article VII - In suits at common law, where the value in controversy shall exceed twenty dollars, the right of trial by jury shall be preserved, and no fact tried by a jury, shall be otherwise re-examined in any Court of the United States, than according to the rule of the common law.

Article VII - Excessive bail shall not be required, nor excessive fines imposed, nor cruel and unusual punishments inflicted.

Article IX - The enumeration in the Constitution of certain rights shall not be construed to deny or disparage others retained by the people.

Article X - The powers not delegated to the United States by the Constitution, nor prohibited by it to the States, are reserved to the States respectively, or to the people.

Of course the existence of such an impressive commitment to individual rights does not, in itself, guarantee that they will be acknowledged. Much depends upon the political climate in which they operate. The Bill of Rights did not do much to advance the position of the American negro for many decades after the abolition of slavery, though eventually it was the judges who, in a series of decisions, did move to ensure that negroes received their 'inalienable rights'.

In one respect, it could be argued that the Bill is a barrier to necessary social advance. The Second Amendment to the Constitution gives Americans the right to bear arms, and any proposed measures of gun-control always founder as opponents assert their constitutional rights.

The phrases of the American Bill of Rights are broad, like those in the European Convention, and require judicial interpretation. Experience has varied, for in some cases rights have not been enforced whereas in others they could be embraced by the vague terminology and put into effect.

France

The French Revolutionaries were inspired by many of the ideas of the fledgeling United States, but the repercussions of what happened in France in 1789 and after had a greater immediate influence, especially throughout Europe.

In 1789 the Declaration of the Rights of Man and Citizens was adopted by the National Assembly at Versailles, and its tone reflects the main ideas of the C18 Enlightenment. These included that

> *men are born free and equal in rights ... the aim of every political association is the preservation of the natural and undoubted rights of men. These rights are liberty, property, security and resistance to oppression.*

The French Revolution was later to deny some of these rights, but the Declaration was to be a basic charter of European liberals for the next fifty years. It was Lord Acton who said that it was 'stronger than all the armies of Napoleon'.

These principles of 1789 were later to enthral and divide the whole of Europe, and few European states were unaffected by what had happened. Many of them incorporated statements of human rights into their own constitutions as did the Swedes in 1809 and Holland in 1815.

Other Examples

More immediately relevant than broad declarations in pursuit of the rights to life, liberty and the pursuit of happiness, however, is the experience of the European Convention. One of its objectives was to work for the 'maintenance and further realisation of human rights and fundamental freedoms'.

Several of the newly independent African nations were to be influenced by this example, whereas the Caribbean states drew more widely upon a number of international statements. By contrast, India, with perhaps the most detailed formulation of rights, was inspired more by British and American legal history.

Chapter Nine

Some Further Points to Consider

1. Entrenchment and Parliamentary Sovereignty

Parliamentary Sovereignty is often portrayed as a corner-stone of our democratic system. As Parliament is sovereign, one Parliament cannot bind succeeding ones. Therein lies a difficulty.

If a Bill of Rights was to be introduced into British law, this could be done in either of two forms. The weaker version would not have a specially privileged status and the Parliament which passes such a Bill could with equal facility amend it. The stronger version includes a fortifying measure; it would be entrenched, and its provisions would take precedence over subsequent statutes and render them invalid if they were inconsistent with it.

Entrenchment could be achieved by some device such as a referendum after an agreed Bill of Rights had been drawn up and Parliament had passed it. An entrenched Bill could only be repealed or amended after some specified procedure had been followed (This could require a two-thirds majority of both Houses or a referendum).

The whole point is that it would be a permanent statute difficult to alter or evade by any incoming government. Such an entrenched Bill would significantly affect the British Constitution for the sovereignty of Parliament would no longer apply in as much as the Bill of Rights would always prevail over any other legislative plans.

Such problems concerning the status of the Bill, whether it should be entrenched or otherwise, would be avoided if we were to incorporate the European Convention. This would have precedence over other legislation in the same way that European Community legislation has precedence following our signing of the European Community Act in 1972.

In this way, the Bill would have priority over other legislation unless Parliament expressly said that a particular piece of legislation derogated from it. Governments would not readily seek to override the Bill of Rights and thereby put themselves in an exposed position. Judges would be the arbiters when other legislation conflicts with the fundamental rights incorporated into British law, and thus judges would be ultimately controlling Parliament.

2.   The Position of Judges

Whether in an entrenched home-grown Bill of Rights or an incorporated European one, the task of deciding whether laws are compatible with the Bill of Rights is thrown on to the judiciary. This involves some transfer of political power from Westminster to the judges, for Parliament's decision-making capacity would be eroded. Some would say that it is precisely because Parliament has not been effective in safeguarding rights that it is necessary to invoke the courts as our protector.

Alarm about giving the courts this important role of interpreting our rights is perhaps the main consideration of opponents. Why should unaccountable judges be any more competent to decide what are inevitably going to be political questions? Judges would enter the political arena in arbitrating between the rights claimed by different groups possessing differing political values.

The fear of judicial power and a suspicion that these judges are likely to veer towards a conservative stance, is at the nub of the controversy. The points about the backgrounds and attitudes of judges may have validity, yet there are several examples when they have been critical of Labour and Conservative governments in their defence of the individual citizen.

Their judgements have by no means all been at the expense of Labour for in several cases since 1979 the Government's proposals have been struck down. The Departments of the Environment, Health and Social Security, and Education have especially been affected in this way. Even in the field of industrial relations, where the Left has many deep-rooted anxieties, by no means every case has been decided against the workers. Some major decisions have certainly been detrimental to the interests of trade unions, but over the years the courts have sometimes come down on the side of labour.

It is also possible that if the European Convention was incorporated, then judges would be more sympathetic to libertarian concerns. Once the Convention was a part of the judicial scenery, and the rights defined a well recognised part of our constitutional law, then, as in the United States, judges might well take up the cudgels on behalf of the aggrieved citizen more than they do today. Indeed, there are already some signs that judges are beginning to reflect European ideas and attitudes in their judgements, attitudes deriving from EC law and the Convention.

Defeat in Strasbourg

Any British government has two basic options if it wishes to escape from the pattern of defeat at Strasbourg. It could remove the right of British individuals to take complaints on human rights to the European Commission, so that in future only the British government would be able to use the Strasbourg machinery. There have been some voices on the Right in recent years which have much lamented Britain's constant rebuffs, and a few calls to withdraw the right of individual petition. However, as on several occasions the procedure has provided a useful remedy against injustices perpetrated by British governments, the loss of this avenue would be much resisted and this option is highly unlikely to be seriously considered.

Alternatively, of course, the Government could incorporate the Convention into British law and thereby avoid the 'rush to Strasbourg' and the indignity which can result.

The Rushdie Affair, 1988-89

The drama surrounding the case of the distinguished literary figure, Salman Rushdie, in early 1989, highlights a problem of free expression already alluded to - namely that the very important right of a person or group to be able to air their ideas can be one which causes grief and hurt to other people.

His controversial book, 'The Satanic Verses', aroused intense hostility from the Muslim community in Britain and, even more significantly, overseas; it was alleged to be a blasphemy against the prophet Mohammed. The Ayatollah Khomeini, the then ruler of Iran and an Islamic fundamentalist, urged that Rushdie be 'sent to hell' (i.e. killed) by loyal Muslims for his gross affront to their deeply-held feelings.

Muslims in Britain, some of whom resorted to a public burning of the book in Bradford in January 1989, want an amendment to the law for only blasphemy against the Christian faith can be dealt with in British courts. Some of them feel that the free circulation of books can be stopped when it suits the British authorities, as in the Spycatcher Case, but when something detrimental to their beliefs is published, there is no law via which their objections can be debated in court.

The 'fatwa' or death sentence has still not been removed, and the present Ayatollah has reiterated its terms which include a bounty of more than $2 million. The threat to Rushdie's life has not diminished, and advocates of free speech in Britain have urged that Britain should take a stronger line with the Iranian Government.

Several left-wing MPs, who have condemned the Fatwa are also uneasy about tensions the book has caused among their Muslim communities, many of whom live in Labour constituencies. For instance, Roy Hattersley has opposed the introduction of a paperback edition of 'The Satanic Verses', whilst abhorring the death threat.

The issue illustrates, if nothing else, the need in society to balance one person's freedom to write against the harm that can be done to community relations when the views expressed are deeply offensive to particular groups and a threat to public order.

Chapter Ten

Recent Concerns

In the last few years, there has been growing anxiety that our rights are being endangered, and some of the cases involving the European Court such as equal pay for women, immigration law and the detention of alleged terrorists have highlighted the concern.

Fear was expressed over the Police Act 1984, allowing the police to detain suspects without charge for 4 days and denying them access to a solicitor for 36 hours. 'Stop and Search' powers were also extended, enabling the police to set up roadblocks; some 70 were erected in the Nottingham area alone, in the Miners' Strike.

That year saw the banning of unions at GCHQ, the intelligence-gathering centre, and those who refused to resign were either later transferred elsewhere or forced to take early retirement (The Government's case has subsequently been upheld by the European Commission).

Also in 1984, prosecutions were brought under the Official Secrets Act against two civil servants, Clive Ponting and Sarah Tisdall, who revealed information gathered in the course of their work. Particularly in the latter case, some claimed this to be an over-reaction as her revelations caused no harm to national security.

'Spycatcher' - A Case Study

Many other cases have arisen since 1984, most notably the 'Spycatcher' saga which began in 1987 as the Government went to enormous lengths to stop people reading Peter Wright's book on the British security services. Some newspapers, notably The Observer, The Sunday Times and The Guardian, were restrained from commenting on aspects of the affair until in October 1988 the House of Lords declared that the Attorney-General was no longer entitled to an injunction.

The issue went to the European Court which gave its verdict in November 1991. The judgement was that in attempting to prevent the three papers from disclosing the evidence of wrongdoing by MI5, the Government had violated Article 10 of the Convention - the one which guarantees freedom of expression and information.

The Court upheld the principle of 'prior restraint', thus supporting the Government's initial injunctions to stop publication of Mr. Wright's allegations. However, it argued that once 'Spycatcher' had been published in the USA in July 1987, the contents were available elsewhere and thus should have been available to the British public.

For the Government the verdict was a blow casting doubt upon the validity of sections of its new Official Secrets Act which has not yet been tested in the courts. Passed during the 'Spycatcher' deliberations, the Act specifically seeks to rule out publication abroad as a defence for publication in Britain. It imposes an absolute duty of silence on members of the security and intelligence services, not just whilst they are in active work but for the rest of their lives. The Court will now need to be satisfied that the Government is taking effective measures to redress its offence against Article 10, and this will involve reviewing the Act.

For civil libertarians, the judgement was disappointing. The European Commission had already ruled against the British Government's 'prior injunction', and the Court reversed this decision. The Commission thought that publication was in the national interest, whereas the Court emphasised the 'national security arguments' which had featured prominently in British discussion of the case. Ten judges disputed the Court's decision to uphold the principle of 'prior restraint', claiming that the Government's original injunctions were 'less a question of the duty of confidentiality than the fear of disclosure of certain irregularities carried out by the Security Service in the pursuit of political rather than intelligence aims'.

The Court did award £100,000 compensation to The Sunday Times, and £50,000 each to The Observer and The Guardian, but the newspapers were disappointed that they won only on the point that the Government was wrong to maintain gagging injunctions once the book was in circulation abroad. 'Prior injunction' has been ruled 'unconstitutional' in the USA and the Court's decision on this suggests that its attitude is cautious and conservative on security matters.

In four key areas, critics alleged that the Government was contemptuous of civil liberties;

1. The Official Secrets Act, 1989

The 1911 Official Secrets Act was widely seen as unworkable, and its infamous 'catch-all' Clause Two forbade any unauthorised disclosure of information even down to such trivial items as a Ministry of Defence luncheon menu! After blocking a Private Member's Bill, the Government produced one which it said was more liberal than the 1911 Act, in that it considerably narrowed the area where disclosure was forbidden.

However, in what it regards as more vital areas, the new measure greatly tightens up the situation. There is now no 'public interest' defence, the one used by Clive Ponting when he was acquitted for revealing secret information over the 'Belgrano' episode. The Act excludes the view that a disclosure revealing fraud, neglect or unlawful activity can be in the public interest.

Critics assert that if people can be prosecuted in the public interest then they must be permitted to defend themselves by citing the public interest. There may be times when to reveal information is the only way to draw attention to a serious threat to public safety. Thus it could be better to expose a major defence scandal, even at the risk of some possible danger to national security. It is a question of balancing the 'public need to know' with the importance of preserving security considerations.

2. The Prevention of Terrorism Act

This has already been referred to in the earlier case study, and whenever the Act comes up for renewal its 'draconian' powers (rejected by the European Court in 1989), are hotly contested. The law was originally rushed through Parliament in 1974 in the wake of the Birmingham 'pub bombings', by a Labour Government. However, Labour has opposed its renewal for ten years and continues to do so. In 1993, sensitive to the gibe that the party opposes every piece of Tory legislation to crack down on hardened criminals, its Front Bench spokesman offered to hold talks with the Home Office to bring about agreed amendments to the Act. The suggestion was turned down. Labour voted against the Government, but the Act was again renewed.

Labour's most serious criticism has centred on the powers to detain suspects in police custody for seven days without trial, the power which attracted the hostile ruling of the European Court. It accepts the idea of detention for up to a week, but believes that an order to extend the period beyond 48 hours should be subject to the judicial review of the courts and not an executive decision made by the Home Secretary. In 1992, 8 suspects were detained beyond 2 days.

Labour is also concerned about 'exclusion orders' under which the Home Secretary can expel someone from Britain to Northern Ireland, or vice versa. As such, these 'internal exile orders', as they are sometimes called, effectively bar some UK citizens in Ulster from travelling to the mainland (81 in 1992).

It is also said that the ratio of charges to arrests shows that too many are held where the case is unlikely to stand up in Court. Out of the 184 Irish 'terrorists' detained in 1987, 176 were released without being prosecuted. In 1992, 160 were detained, all but 20 in connection with Northern Irish terrorism; of those detained, 41 were either charged or deported.

Furthermore, there are doubts about the value of statements produced towards the end of a 7-day detention, and the no-jury Diplock courts have tended to place less emphasis on confessions which could have resulted from duress.

The arguments on either side were rehearsed again in early 1994 in a Parliamentary debate on the renewal of the measure. Labour opposed renewal and was accused of being unwilling to will the means to defeat terrorism.

3. The Right to Silence

As part of its package of measures to deal with the terrorist threat in Northern Ireland, the Government limited the right of silence of the accused. No-one can force the suspect to speak, but whereas previously the judge could not infer guilt if the right was exercised, the silence can now be taken into consideration when the question of innocence or guilt is being debated. Anyone who stays silent throughout is now taking a significant risk.

The Home Secretary announced that this change in the law will eventually be extended to the rest of the UK for the Government felt that the accused currently has too much of an advantage over those prosecuting. To his opponents, this seemed a serious blow to the traditional presumption that a person is innocent until proven to be guilty.

In 1994, despite the findings of the Runciman Commission on Criminal Justice, the Major Government has introduced new legislation to end the existing situation. The right to silence is in a sense bound to remain; no-one can be forced to answer questions. In the future, however, the court will be able to infer guilt from a defendant's refusal to answer in a police station.

'Libertarian' groups on the Centre-Left see this as a serious and unnecessary erosion of liberty. They hold that there is little evidence of such silence impeding the conviction of terrorists or other serious criminals, and that the measure is draconian and unfair; silence at a police station, under heavy and intimidatory questioning, might be the natural course for people overwhelmed by the circumstances.

Some lawyers believe that the Government's move could eventually backfire, for it could be incompatible with the European Convention; Article 6 guarantees that defendents should be presumed innocent until proven guilty, and the right to a free trial. They cite a case brought against France, in which the Court judged that any person charged with a criminal offence had the right to remain silent and not to incriminate himself. Also, they point to the fact that the European Commission has already ruled admissible two UK cases concerning the denial of the right of silence, one of which relates to the procedure operating in Northern Ireland since 1988.

4. The Media

The Government has leaned heavily on the media to get controversial programmes banned, delayed or modified. 'Real Lives' in 1985 (containing an interview with a Sinn Fein representative), the 'Secret Society' programme on the Zircon spy satellite, in 1987 the radio series 'My Country Right or Wrong', and, in 1988, the ITV documentary 'Death on the Rock', were all initially stopped and then later broadcast (sometimes in an amended form). In the case of the latter, the Government wanted it postponed until after the trial of those involved in the Gibraltar shootings.

In late 1988, the Government banned radio and TV interviews with spokesmen for Sinn Fein, the UDA and the paramilitaries. Programmes could include the 'reported speech' of such supporters, or an actor's voice could read a quotation, but members of these organisations were unable to speak for themselves fairly.

As Sinn Fein had an MP until 1992 (and still has more than 50 local councillors), this was and remains a serious limitation upon their work which often has nothing to do with the question of security, but is concerned with constituency business. The Government claimed that people found the appearance of Sinn Feiners on television offensive, and was keen to deny them the 'oxygen of publicity'.

The Government of the Irish Republic lifted its ban on Sinn Fein and paramilitary spokesmen in January 1994, after prolonged pressure. The BBC responded by restating its view that the broadcasting restriction prevented it from informing viewers and listeners fully and fairly. Moreover, it pointed out that viewers and listeners in Northern Ireland can now hear interviews on Irish television and radio which they cannot hear on the BBC.

All these areas show how inroads have been made into our traditional freedoms. The charge levelled against the Government was that after more than a decade of rule, it had become arrogant and insensitive to libertarian concerns. It conceded that some peripheral limitations had been imposed but argued that these are dangerous times, that security is the guarantee of our freedom and that faced with great problems of terrorism, special measures are necessary and justifiable. In other words, the relationship between the state and the individual has to be adjusted from time to time to reflect changing circumstances in society.

A Conservative Response

The differing Conservative views as to which are our most important freedoms is seen in the way Government spokesmen frequently say how much they have extended the rights of British people - to own their own council house, buy shares, keep more of the money they earn and decide, as trade unionists, whether they wish to strike and who shall be their leaders.

In particular, Mrs. Thatcher (in Feb. 1989) counter attacked on the charge that the Government was becoming increasingly authoritarian, and spoke of her belief in 'devolution to the individual citizen'. Arguing that ordinary people were fit to run their own lives, more so than politicians, she cited many of the changes above, adding denationalisation, and devolving power to tenants, parents and NHS patients.

Her concept of freedom did not extend, however, to support for the European 'Charter for Social Rights' of 1989, which the British Government, alone among EC members, refused to sign. This Charter provided for guaranteed worker participation and the right to strike, as well as strong health and safety measures throughout the Community. She reacted sharply against this 'socialist charter' which would have allowed 'socialism to creep back into Britain by the back door'; it embraced policies which she had legislated to remove from the statute book (At the Maastricht Summit of December 1991, John Major, the new Prime Minister, secured an opt-out from what became the Social Chapter; the other eleven representatives gave it their approval).

His Government, looking for a popular centrepiece for the Conservative programme, introduced as its 'big idea' the Citizen's Charter. This gives members of the public additional rights as consumers; for instance, they are entitled to expect trains to run approximately on time and hospital treatment to be offered within a reasonable period. If the public services fail to deliver, they are liable to pay compensation. The Charter is a code of good practice aiming to promote more efficient and user-friendly public services, offering guaranteed standards in areas such as education, local government, the postal services and the railways.

Such ideas are said to derive from an American business book 'In Search of Excellence', in which quality is defined as offering customers what they really want. Some private firms on both sides of the Atlantic have attempted to achieve consumer satisfaction in this way. Labour produced its own adaptation of this formula with its proposed customer service contract in 1986. It claimed that the Prime Minister had borrowed its ideas, and that as the public services were starved of funds the likelihood of achieving significant improvements was seriously diminished.

All of the main parties have shown interest in this field of 'customer satisfaction', an indication of how wide ranging is the discussion of people's entitlements. However, the approach of the Citizen's Charter is a limited one, promising a better deal for members of the public. The Government has little to say on any constitutional changes designed to bring about a fundamental change in the relationship of the individual to the state.

Charter 88, and its Supporters

Mrs. Thatcher's defence of her Government's record does not convince those people alarmed by what they see as a growth in governmental power at the expense of personal freedom. 'Liberty', formerly the 'National Council for Civil Liberties', launched an advertising campaign enumerating countless ways in which it felt that people's rights had been trampled on since 1979. In November 1988, a new organisation, Charter 88, launched a campaign for constitutional reform. Among the reforms it wanted, such as a change in the electoral system and a new Second Chamber, a key requirement was a Bill of Rights.

Many people, writers, artists and politicians to the left of the Conservative Party, signed the Charter; they were worried that our rights no longer seem inviolable, and argue that they need to be enshrined as part of a written constitution. They want to see the European Convention incorporated, believing that such a measure would give citizens a clearer idea of their liberties and also serve as an educational force to ensure that the next generation comes to learn what are generally agreed rights. Above all, minorities and disadvantaged people would be better protected.

Labour's Changing Approach

In 1990, Labour published 'The Charter of Rights', its programme designed to guarantee individual liberty in a free society. It promised to 'restore those freedoms which have been lost during the last decade, and ... create, in law, new rights ... By setting out these rights in individual and specific Acts of Parliament, we shall establish them in law as available to every British citizen'. It proposed new rights on such matters as freedom of information, privacy and control of the security services.

It spoke of using its proposed Second Chamber as a guarantor of these rights, to prevent their easy repeal by some hostile or even authoritarian government. Rights were to be safeguarded by allowing the new body to delay any repeal measure for the lifetime of a Parliament. This would give the electorate the chance to determine whether they wished that government to stay in power and allow its wishes to be implemented. This delaying power would apply to any rights designated as 'fundamental', and would be a means of entrenching key parts of the Charter.

The Party Conference had already rejected the idea of incorporating the European Convention into British law, and saw difficulties with the whole idea of a Bill of Rights. The opposition had centred on three main points;

1. That a Bill setting out broad principles would have to be interpreted by the courts.

2. That its general provisions would offer only a limited protection of rights, and that, once introduced, its supporters would see it as adequate by itself. It might have some value for the prosperous and articulate members of society who could afford to take legal action, but for most people the Charter offered a more positive programme.

3. That there was no catalogue of rights to which all could subscribe. There is an ideological dimension to the discussion, for Left and Right see the question very differently. This applies particularly when rights conflict, such as the rights of a tenant and his/her landlord. Faced by making choices when rights collide, the likelihood is that any statement would consist of vacuous generalisations to accommodate everyone.

Roy Hattersley, the Deputy Leader until 1992, was seen as hostile to any Bill of Rights. It was, therefore, rather surprising when, in mid-1991, he appeared to change his position and offer modified support for what he would 'loosely call a Bill of Rights'. He remained opposed to the European Convention, 'for the principles ... it sets out are so general that they are often meaningless and are then almost qualified out of existence by sub-clauses that try to make the principles a practical legal prospect'.

His conversion rested on three 'increasingly attractive' arguments;

1. Support for a Bill would indicate the sincerity of Labour's commitment to the cause of the citizen's rights.

2. Such a Bill might help to set the climate of opinion, the right ideological mood, in which to legislate for individual rights.

3. A Bill could fill in the gaps, protecting those freedoms for which there was no specific legislation.

Speaking personally and not officially, he saw value in setting out a general statement of principles which could be called a Bill of Rights as that term has a popular appeal. The document would co-exist with Labour's more detailed proposals; the specific legislation would have precedence, but the general framework 'would guide and govern the courts where, and only where, the specific law was silent'.

His 'conversion' was greeted with scepticism by some enthusiasts for a Bill of Rights for they would elevate it to a much more overriding status, seeing it as a pronouncement to which all legislation should conform. However, his remarks indicated some movement in the Labour position, and were an attempt to identify Labour more clearly with the protection of basic rights.

In its 1992 Manifesto, Labour promised that its Charter of Rights would 'establish in law the specific rights of every citizen'. It offered a series of laws to protect the rights of minorities and those who suffer injustice; for instance it wished to strengthen the law on racial discrimination, introduce fair immigration and citizenship laws, and initiate new legislation on women. As part of this programme of positive rights, the disabled were to be included in the anti-discriminatory safeguards.

John Smith spoke sympathetically about the European Convention at the time of his election to the leadership later that year. In March 1993, he reversed almost five decades of Labour opposition to a British Bill of Rights by committing himself to such a measure, through incorporation of the European Convention into British law. In his speech to a Charter 88 meeting he pledged his party to a 'Human Rights Act' to protect the rights of the individual against state institutions. He said,

I wish to see a fundamental shift in the balance of power between the people and the state - a shift away from an over-powering state to citizen's democracy where people have rights and powers, and where they are served by accountable and responsive government.

The speech itself marked a 'fundamental shift', for Labour had writhed long and hard before its conversion. It has always disliked the fact that the Convention gives priority to individual rights over collective principles. Mr. Smith has made a break with this philosophy, but has not shown any eagerness to embrace the draft Bill of Rights produced by the IPPR (below) which, it is argued, improves on the European model by preventing the courts from directly interfering with broad social programmes like abortion.

The Liberty Solution

In November 1991, at a convention organised by Charter 88, the aim was to find a consensus between those organisations committed to more protection for our liberties. Those at the meeting examined draft constitutions submitted by the left-wing think tank, the Institute for Public Policy Research, the pro-Tory Institute for Economic affairs, the Liberal Democrats and Tony Benn, Labour MP. The first three support, in varying degrees, the incorporation of the European Convention and/or the enactment of a British Bill of Rights arbitrated by a Supreme Court and amendable only by a two-thirds majority in Parliament.

The role of judges in interpreting a Bill of Rights proved to be the key issue. Labour Party representatives made it clear that they could not support a document in which the final say was left in the hands of the judiciary rather than of Parliament. The IPPR draft had suggested that reform of the selection and training of the judges could be the answer, so that the judiciary would become more progressive in character. A Judicial Appointments Commission, comprising legal and lay representatives, would pay particular attention to matters of race and gender. Having a more representative judiciary would help to create 'a culture in which the protection of rights is central to our law, where people know their rights and can claim them'.

Some Labour supporters were more willing to consider the Bill of Rights published by Liberty. In this version, the distinctive feature is that judges would not have the final say in defining civil and political rights. A borderline case could be referred back to a scrutiny committee of the House of Commons which would be able to override the judge if there was any disagreement about the political meaning, as opposed to the judicial interpretation, of an issue.

The twenty rights set out in this 'People's Charter' are set out in much more detail than usual (118 pages!), so that there is amplification of what each one involves. For instance, the 'right to life' is not left open to interpretation in different circumstances, but made specific; the death penalty for treason or piracy would be repealed, but abortion would still be allowed.

Liberty hoped that its approach could win over the support of all those who wanted to see protection for rights, but who were anxious about too much influence being placed in the hands of the judiciary. Civil libertarians argue that in too many cases judges have failed to challenge abuses of executive power.

Signatories of the Charter, and all others concerned about our liberty, believe that when rights are taken from some, the freedom of all is threatened. Broad agreement on that point, however, conceals very different views as to what the basic rights are and how they are best enforced.

Some Relevant Quotations

Quintin Hogg, 1977, 'New Charter'

> *I know, of course, that the traditional English view has been that remedies are more important than rights. Until recently I agreed with this ... but I have changed my mind ... the old remedies have proved inadequate in practice .... It is the arbitrary rule of the modern Parliament itself which needs discussion.*

Lord Hailsham, 1976, 'Dimbleby Lecture'

> *So, the sovereignty of Parliament has increasingly become, in practice the sovereignty of the Commons, and the sovereignty of the Commons has increasingly become the sovereignty of the government, which in addition to its influence in Parliament, controls the party whips, the party machine and the Civil Service. This means that what has always been an elective dictatorship in theory, but one in which the component parts operated in practice to control one another, has become a machine in which one of those parts has come to exercise a predominant influence over the rest.*

Michael Zander, 1985, 'New Society'

> *The main argument for a Bill of Rights is, after all, that it strengthens the citizen's hand against government and other public authorities ... The range of alternative means open to the citizen with a grievance are feeble by comparison - letters to the editor or to one's MP, appeals to the minister or his civil servants, marching and*

demonstrating.   None of these normally brings home much bacon.

Guardian, 1976, Editorial

There is no fundamental objection to a Bill of Rights, it could have positive results.   Above all, it would re-emphasise the rights of the individual against the state which are always in danger of erosiion.   But too much store should not be set by it. It would at best be a collection of valuable truisms, but at worse it could be a dangerous cosmetic.

Lord Denning, 1977, House of Lords Debate (on incorporation of the European Convention)

The bill would mean that judges would have to hear millions of cases brought by a lot of crack-pots.

Lord Lloyd, 1976, House of Lords

The fact of the matter is ... that the law cannot be a substitute for politics.   The political decisions must be taken by politicians. In a society like ours that means by people who are removable.

Margaret Thatcher, 1988, House of Commons

I do not think it right to incorporate that Convention into our law.

Margaret Thatcher, 1989, House of Commons

(of the Rushdie affair); Freedom of speech and expression is subject only to the laws of this land, in particular libel and blasphemy, and will remain subject to the rule of law. It is fundamental to everything in which we believe and cannot be interfered with, by any outside force.

Finally, two different views of our freedoms after a decade of Thatcherite rule, from firstly the Home Secretary of the time and then from his 'shadow'.

Douglas Hurd, 1989, House of Commons

> *In many different ways, we have added to the liberties of the British people. I feel like a Chancellor of the Exchequer who abolished every tax except two or three, and was then roundly abused for having introduced these two or three.*

Roy Hattersley, 1989, House of Commons

> *Freedom for Mrs. Thatcher is the freedom of the individual to prosper at the expense of the community.*

Some Likely Examination Questions

1. Do you think that the rights of the citizen are adequately protected in Britain? If not, what improvements could be made?

2. How true is it to say that the freedoms of the British people rest on insecure foundations?

3. In what ways have the Conservative Administrations since 1979 changed the relationship between the state and the individual citizen?

4. 'Democracy requires the fullest freedom of expression'. Do we have this in Britain today?

5. Examine the main issues concerning civil liberties in contemporary Britain. How adequately can the courts defend these liberties?

6. 'Britain is one of the few democratic countries which does not have a Bill of Rights to provide redress for its citizens'. Does this matter?

7. Is it feasible to produce a Bill of Rights for Britain?

8. Why have all recent governments resisted any attempts to introduce a Bill of Rights in Britain?

9. Examine the case for incorporating the European Convention on Human Rights into British law. Why has the case not so far been conceded?

10. Do we need a British Bill of Rights when British citizens can take their grievances to the European Court in Strasbourg?

11. How useful is the European Court of Human Rights as a means of gaining redress for aggrieved British citizens?

12. Why does the idea of a Bill of Human Rights have more appeal to liberals than to socialists?

13. 'A Bill of Rights and proportional representation are procedures designed to blunt the cutting edge of socialism'. Discuss.